From Chaos To Clarity

Transforming Pain Into Purpose

Dr. Maria L. Rodriguez

Copyright © 2025
All Rights Reserved

Dedication

For my beloved son, my daughter, and my mother—this book is for you. Your love and strength have been my foundation, and I dedicate this journey to you.

Acknowledgment

I am deeply grateful to those who walked alongside me on this journey. To my friends and family, especially my children and my mother—your presence has been a light during my darkest moments.

To the mentors and therapists who guided me, thank you for your wisdom, compassion, and belief in my healing.

To my readers, whose support and shared experiences have given this book purpose—your encouragement reminds me why stories like ours matter. This book would not exist without each of you, and I am profoundly thankful for your love and support.

About the Author

Dr. Maria Rodriguez is a Licensed Professional Counselor, mental health advocate, and best-selling author renowned for her dedication to helping individuals navigate life's challenges. With over two decades of experience, she is celebrated for her compassion-first approach, empowering clients to heal from trauma and rebuild their lives.

Dr. Rodriguez's exceptional contributions to mental health have earned her numerous accolades, including recognition as one of New Jersey's Top Women Leaders and being named among the Top 25 Executives of New Jersey. She is also a Global Outstanding Leader in Health Care, reflecting her commitment to excellence and transformative care.

Inspired by her personal journey of resilience, Dr. Rodriguez founded counseling centers designed to provide hope and support to individuals and families in need. Through this book, she invites readers to believe in their own strength and embrace the transformative power of hope, healing, and perseverance.

Preface

When I began my journey of healing, I never imagined that I would one day share my story with the world. Yet, as I faced and overcame my own struggles, I realized how many others might be walking a similar path. This book is my way of reaching out to you, the reader, in hopes that my experiences might offer comfort or simply provide a reminder that you are not alone. My life's hardships made me stronger and motivated me to establish counseling centers dedicated to helping others find their way. Healing is possible, and I hope that by reading this book, you find strength in knowing that life's hardest moments can be overcome and that on the other side of pain, there is always a way forward.

Contents

Dedication i

Acknowledgment ii

About The Author iii

Preface iv

Chapter 1: In The Beginning 1

Chapter 2: The Divorce 3

Chapter 3: Hopeless 13

Chapter 4: Divorce And Its Impacts On A Child's Mind 21

Chapter 5: Understanding The Trauma 30

Chapter 6: Communicating With Your Child 41

Chapter 7: Helping Your Child Cope 51

Chapter 8: How Can You Cope? 61

Chapter 9: The Bright Side 71

Chapter 10: Healing From It All 81

Chapter 1: In the Beginning

"Children don't care about child support battles or who loves whom less. They care that their parents show up, especially at the moments that matter. When there's a Christmas recital, and they peek through the curtain, they hope to see everyone they love sitting together without fighting. This was the childhood I longed for but never had."

I can't stress enough how accurately Jessica James, an aspiring playwright and actress, spelled out my feelings with those words. I experienced the fallout of my parents' separation beginning when I was two years old. Although they officially divorced later, their tumultuous relationship persisted for two years after I was born. Even though I have taken the hard step of forgiving them—a step that set me free in many ways—it doesn't erase the reality that the divorce still hurts. After 40 years, it still does.

Now that I'm an adult, I understand the reasons, but does that ease my pain? Definitely not! I still wish that my mom and dad were married. I wish time travel was possible so I could go back and fix their relationship before the disaster happened, so I wouldn't have to split holidays. Both my parents may have healed, but the deep wounds inflicted upon me persist to this day. Yes, I am a child of divorced parents, but before I go deeper into how it all happened and the impact it had on my life, it's important to shed some light on my background, including who I am, where I come from, and so on. Life in the Dominican Republic during my parents' upbringing was far from simple. The political turmoil of the 1960s, however, cast a long shadow over their lives. My mother's father, who worked for the government, lived in constant fear as the political climate turned volatile. This fear became a reality when the assassination of the country's president led to a wave of retaliation against anyone associated with the regime.

My mother's survival hinged on a heartbreaking choice to leave her family and her homeland for safety in the United States, a journey marked by sacrifice and loss that echoed through our lives. For my father's family, survival meant adaptation. My grandfather, threatened by the incoming regime, made the life-altering decision to change our family name from Maldonado to Rodriguez, a choice that ultimately saved their lives.

This legacy of resilience and reinvention shaped my parents in profound ways. Their survival amidst the chaotic conditions of their homeland instilled a fierce determination, but it also carried an invisible weight. The same strength that allowed them to endure such hardship became a quiet strain on their marriage. What started as a vibrant union gradually fractured under the emotional burdens of their past, leaving cracks that shaped not only their lives but the foundation of my childhood.

Chapter 2: The Divorce

My father was a man born for the spotlight. He was the kind of person who could walk into a room and instantly become the center of attention. With a smile that could light up a cloudy day and a gift of gab that could charm a snake out of its hole, he was a natural-born salesman.

Back in the day, when music came in big, round black discs and you needed a record player to play them, my dad was the king. He'd pack up his suitcase full of these records, each one a tiny world of sounds, and go door to door, spreading the joy of music. He was like a traveling minstrel, but instead of a lute, he carried a collection of tunes.

My mother had just landed in the United States after escaping the turmoil in the Dominican Republic when she first encountered my father. It was on one of his musical missions that fate stepped in. She was minding her own business, probably dreaming of faraway places or delicious cakes, when there was a knock at her door.

Standing on her doorstep was my dad, all smiles and shining shoes. At that moment, something clicked. It was like a spark ignited, a sudden burst of color in a black-and-white world. For him, it was love at first sight. She? Well, she was intrigued.

He didn't give up easily. Like a determined puppy, he kept coming back, his suitcase full of melodies and his heart full of hope. With each visit, he painted a picture of a world filled with music and magic. He was like a magician pulling rabbits out of a hat, except instead of rabbits, he was offering a world of sound. Slowly, my mother's heart began to soften. She found herself looking forward to his visits, drawn in by his charm and his endless supply of stories.

Their love story began like a vibrant melody, full of hope and harmony. Inseparable, they found joy in each other's company, creating a beautiful duet that transformed their world. As they married, their hearts brimmed with dreams of a lifetime filled with laughter and a love that would endure. But as the years went by, dissonance crept in, and the enchanting symphony they once played together gave way to a discordant reality.

What began as subtle critiques soon escalated to acts of control and violence. My mother often described her life as a tightrope walk, with my father's temper threatening to snap the balance at any moment. The smallest misstep, a glance in the wrong direction, a second of inattention, could spark his rage. One day, on a crowded train, a fleeting glance at the platform led to a public slap that shattered her spirit.

This event, however, marked the onset of violence, and it only escalated from there, a dark undercurrent that pulsed through their home. Alcohol became his accelerant, fueling his temper into dangerous explosions. My mother would recount how she'd rush to hide my sister and brother in the closet, their innocent childhoods shielded by a thin wooden door from the terrifying world outside. The house became a fortress under siege, every corner echoing with tension. Fear was a constant companion, a cold hand that gripped her heart.

Isolation was another weapon my father used against her. He cut her off from her friends, poisoning her mind with accusations of betrayal. They were no longer confidantes but potential threats; their friendship, as he would describe, was a mask for hidden desires. The world shrank for my mother, confining her to a prison of his making.

One night, the terror reached its peak. It was the night when he came home in a drunken rage, armed with a gun. He aimed his fury at my mother, his voice a venomous hiss as he unleashed a torrent of threats and accusations at her. Even his own mother could not quell his rage. When she tried to intervene, he turned the gun on her without hesitation. The look in his eyes was wild, unhinged—a stark contrast to the man I once knew as my father.

Finally, my mom found the courage to leave. When she finally took the decision, she hoped the nightmare would end for good. But for my mother, the worst was yet to come. My father's violent outbursts didn't stop—he broke into our home, wielding the same menacing gun he had used before. He cornered her, threatening her with words that cut like knives.

In a moment of despair, my mother made a desperate choice. Consumed by hopelessness and seeing no other way out, she swallowed a large amount of rat poison. The consequences were immediate and dire. She was rushed to the hospital and spent agonizing days in the intensive care unit, fighting for her life.

Somehow, she pulled through. It was then that life, with its cruel twists, dealt her another unexpected blow: she became pregnant again. It was a shock to everyone, especially since she and Dad had only been intimate once before she left for the Dominican Republic to recover.

Her health took a turn for the worse while she was away. Alone and scared, she ended up in a hospital there. That's when she found out she was pregnant with me. The doctors told her she needed better care, so she came back to the United States. The final months of her pregnancy were spent in a hospital in New York City. After a tough pregnancy, I was finally born on December 8th. But our story didn't have a happy, fairytale beginning. Mom was still very sick, and we were separated right after I was born. To make things even harder, she fainted during childbirth, showing just how much stress her body had been through. Despite these challenges, her relationship with my father continued for two more tumultuous years after my birth.

Once my mother was out of the hospital, the cycle of abuse that had paused momentarily due to childbirth resumed once again. Finally, there came a time when my mother decided she had had enough. I was just a toddler then, barely able to walk when my world turned upside down. My mom packed up our lives with my two older siblings and moved us to a new place. It was like starting over, a fresh beginning in a strange land. She worked hard, day and night, to give us a better life. She was a mom and a dad to us, strong and loving.

Balancing full-time work and the responsibilities of single motherhood, my mother showed incredible strength and determination. She rented an apartment in New York City, and we moved in. In the weeks that followed, we lived in tranquility until my mom made a mistake that she regretted for the rest of her life. Understanding the importance of our father's presence in our lives, she dropped me and my brother to my father's home so we could meet him and maybe spend some quality time together. But, by the time she returned to pick us up, we were gone. As she explained to me later, she was told that we were not home. As ridiculous as it sounds, we were not home for the following seven years, and I didn't see her until the age of nine.

We had been moved to the Dominican Republic. Being a kid, I was excited to be in a new place as I jumped on the sofa in our new home. But I had absolutely no idea what was happening to me: I was being deprived of my mother's love.

My mother, determined to find us, traveled to the Dominican Republic. She stalked the house for hours, waiting to catch a glimpse of us like a detective on a mission. When she finally saw us playing in the yard, it was like a dream come true. She ran towards us, her arms outstretched. I was so small, but I knew she was my mom. I clung to her desperately, afraid to let go. It was like finding a lost piece of myself.

My dad, seeing this reunion, lost control. He tried to pull us away, but I held on tighter. At that moment, I was a tiny warrior protecting my mom. I remember her shirt ripping, buttons flying everywhere. It was scary and confusing, but I knew I had to stay with her. Little did I know that this would be the last time I would see my mom for a long time.

I was too young to understand what divorce meant, but I could feel the storm that was raging around me. My dad's heart was a battlefield, and my mom was the enemy.

His stories about her were varied, for at other times, he mentioned that she was dead or that she left us to rot in the garbage can, that we should be grateful that he was there for us.

Sometimes, my grandma came to live with us, bringing a sense of calm to our chaotic world. She was like a warm blanket on a cold night, offering comfort and love. But even she couldn't stay forever. When she left, it felt like a part of me was leaving, too. I was alone in a house filled with shadows, a small boat adrift in a stormy sea.

Her visits were like brief escapes to a sunny island. I felt loved and safe in her arms, but those moments were fleeting. Whenever she would leave, I would go back to the cold reality, a lonely child longing for a love that felt out of reach.

On most of the days, I felt alone and would cry for hours. My father would stay with us for about 1 to 2 months and suddenly leave without letting us know. His departures would happen at night, or when we were at school, so we couldn't see him leaving. It was truly painful to see my father pack his suitcase to return to the US. When I'd start crying, he would lie that he was not going to leave. I would make him promise that he'd be at home when I returned from school. But by the time I'd come back, he'd be long gone.

Once he would leave, I wouldn't see my father for months. At six years old, I didn't understand what I was feeling, only that it was unbearable. I would lie awake at night, the loneliness pressing down like a heavy blanket, and wonder if there was a place where the pain would stop. For a child, thoughts of heaven weren't about religion or eternity; they were about escape, a fleeting hope for peace in a world that felt so cruelly empty.

It wasn't until years later, with the help of therapy and the hard-won lessons of adulthood, that I realized what those moments had truly taught me. Surviving them was my first act of resilience, even if it didn't feel like it at the time. The child who once thought of escape found the strength to hold on, and that strength would carry me through the challenges yet to come.

Growing up, I had no birthday celebrations, no holidays, no traditions, no sense of unity of family, and no protection.

Even during my father's visits, he would have different girlfriends, whom, at that time, I thought were babysitters. When dad would break up with them, those women would leave, and my relationship with them would come to an end.

Growing up with divorced parents was really tough for me. I had to deal with lots of confusing feelings, and my father's actions only added to the turmoil. One summer, he took me out; I was constantly hoping that we'd have a great time together. But instead, he started saying really mean stuff about my mom that stuck with me. All the happy memories I was hoping to make were now tainted by the hurtful words he said about her.

During that summer, my dad made it his mission to change my perception of my mother. He started poisoning my mind against her, and he told me all these awful stories, like how she didn't care about me or didn't want us to be together as a family anymore.

I had no other option but to believe everything my dad had said to me, even when it hurt to think that a mother could do such a thing to their child. I couldn't understand why my mom would leave me behind and why she chose to be absent from my life. That persistent feeling of sadness engulfed me, and I felt like an unwanted burden, like she didn't love me. My dad's stories made my mom seem like a bad, heartless person, and it added to my pain.

I didn't understand the purpose of the narrative my dad was feeding us. He had our custody, but that wasn't enough for him. He wanted me to forget about my mom completely.

They call it parental alienation; it's a form of emotional abuse, which is when one parent manipulates and tries to make you hate the other parent. My dad was really angry at my mom, and he told me all these negative things about her to paint a distorted image of my mother. I was too young to know the truth, so I believed everything he said. As I got older, I felt this emptiness inside me, like I was missing something important—deep down, I knew it was mother's love. I'd see other kids with their moms, laughing and having fun, and it made me feel even lonelier. I kept wondering why my mom didn't want me, why she left me, or at least that's what my dad told me.

My dad did everything to keep me away from my mom. He made sure I didn't try to contact her, instilling in my young mind the idea that she didn't care about me. He manipulated me and made me think she was the actual villain in our story, which I would find out years later wasn't the case.

Deep down, I always had this nagging feeling, a tiny doubt that made me question everything. I'd look at old photos, recall all the memories I shared with my mother, searching for answers in those frozen faces. Was my mom really the person my dad said she was? Or was there more to the story that he wasn't telling me? The nine years I spent away from my mother were the hardest of my young life. Her absence left a void in me that nothing else could fill. I yearned for her every single day, yet I couldn't remember what she looked like, the sound of her voice, or the warmth of her embrace. The ache of longing became a constant companion, a wound that refused to heal.

Chapter 3: Hopeless

"Even when it feels hopeless. Like everything is telling him to let go. This time, maybe this time, he won't let go. He'll just... hold on, and he'll keep going. He'll keep going until he sees the sun."

- Val Emmich

Looking back, it's difficult to put into words the depth of emotions that accompanied me throughout the challenging early years of my life. The absence of my mother's love left a permanent void in my heart, a yearning for nurturing and affection that seemed insurmountable at times. I was the younger one, four years behind my brother.

Growing up, it felt like I had to learn how to take care of myself almost from the start. Dad was hardly ever there. He was like a ghost in our house, quiet and distant. And then there was his girlfriend. She was supposed to be the grown-up, the one who looked after us. But most of the time, it felt like she was just there like a useless piece of furniture that didn't do much.

With time, I got used to figuring things out on my own. Making sure there was food to eat wasn't always easy, but I learned to find ways. Our home was often a crazy mess, so I tried to bring a little bit of order to my own world.

Growing up without birthdays, holidays, or the warmth of family traditions left me feeling invisible. My survival became a daily act of creating order amidst chaos. I found solace in routine, my brother's laughter, and the imaginary world I crafted among flowers, my secret companions when reality was too harsh to bear.

Those early years taught me a hard lesson: I couldn't rely on anyone but myself. I had built a wall around my heart, a way to protect myself from getting hurt again. That feeling, that I'm the only one I can truly count on, has stayed with me well into adulthood. It's part of who I am now.

Despite the tough times we faced growing up, my brother always seemed to find peace in the most unexpected places. Sports became his escape from the turmoil that surrounded us at home. He threw himself into every game with a passion. From dawn till dusk, he could be found on the makeshift field in our neighborhood, playing soccer or basketball with the other kids. It was there, amidst the shouts and laughter, that he could momentarily forget the instability that plagued our family life.

In addition to sports, my brother had another outlet: art. It was a surprising passion that blossomed quietly amidst the chaos. He had a knack for drawing, especially superheroes and fantastical worlds. I remember watching him hunched over his sketchbook for hours, completely absorbed in his creations. His sketches were intricate and detailed, each stroke of the pencil a testament to his imagination.

I was always amazed at how he could balance sports and art with everything else going on in our lives. Maybe that's why he loved them so much – they were like two sides of a coin, helping him find a balance. The rush of the game and the quiet peace of drawing were like yin and yang for him.

For me, things were different. I felt lost and alone a lot of the time. It was like I was stuck in a dark place, and I couldn't find my way out. To cope, I created my own special world in my head. I imagined a place filled with beautiful flowers that were my friends. I talked to them, and it felt like they understood me in a way that no one else could. It was my secret garden where I could hide from the pain of feeling misunderstood.

Writing soon became another refuge for my emotions. I started keeping a journal, pouring out my innermost thoughts, fears, and dreams onto the pages. It became a safe haven, a private space where I could be completely honest with myself without fear of judgment. In those pages, I found solace in expressing what I couldn't say out loud, a way to make sense of the turmoil within me.

Despite these outlets, there were nights when the weight of my emotions felt unbearable. I would lie awake, tears streaming down my face, longing for a sense of belonging and love that seemed so elusive. It was during these moments that my fantasies and writing became even more important, guiding me through the darkest of times.

Through it all, I learned that sometimes, the imaginary worlds we create and the words we write can be our greatest companions. They offer us a lifeline when everything else feels overwhelming. In the depths of my loneliness, I discovered a resilience within myself – a strength to navigate the complexities of my emotions and find moments of peace amidst the storm.

Even though I could escape into my own made-up world, our real life was far from perfect. It felt like our home was always changing. It was a constant spin of new women. Each one brought a different set of rules, like puzzle pieces that never quite fit. My brother and I were the lost pawns in this endless game, forced to adapt and readjust with every new player. It was as if we were living in a world without solid ground, where nothing felt permanent or safe.

I longed for stability, for someone to anchor us, but instead, we were adrift in a sea of uncertainty. It was hard to connect with anyone when you were always bracing yourself for the next change. The laughter and warmth of childhood were replaced by a cold, unfamiliar routine. My life felt like a never-ending game of musical chairs. Just when I thought I was getting used to one person being around, they were gone, replaced by someone completely different. It was like living in a constant state of limbo, never knowing what to expect next. Every new girlfriend Dad brought home meant learning new rules, adjusting to different moods, and trying to figure out where I fit in. It was exhausting and confusing, and it made it really hard to feel settled or connected to anyone.

Then came the final blow. One of these women became my father's wife, and with her came a world of silence. The vibrant colors of our old life were drained, replaced by the stark, colorless existence of a Jehovah's Witness house hold. No more birthdays, no holidays, no simple joys to look forward to. It felt like someone had stolen the last pieces of our childhood, leaving us feeling empty and alone.

The truth is, I was starved for love. My father was lost in a storm of bitterness, his heart a frozen wasteland. He couldn't give what he didn't have. And his partners? Indifference was their middle name, their occasional cruelty, a sharp sting in an already aching heart. As for my mother, she was a fading memory, her love a distant star twinkling in the night sky of my mind.

I felt like a ghost drifting through life, unseen, unheard. A child yearning for warmth, for a touch of kindness, for the simple feeling of being loved. But these were foreign concepts in our home. I was a barren field, longing for the rain of affection, but the skies above remained stubbornly dry.

Despite the chaos at home, school offered a strange kind of comfort. There was a routine, a schedule. Things happened in a predictable order. My favorite place to be was in the world of books and history. Lost in a story or exploring a distant time, I could forget about everything else.

But even in this safe space, I struggled. I was just an average student, never really shining. The noise in my head, caused by the troubles at home, often drowned out the teacher's voice. Sometimes, I'd try to join in, to be part of things. Drama club and choir – these were my attempts to escape, to find a place where I belonged. But it was hard to feel like I truly fit in anywhere.

The biggest problem was me. I didn't like myself very much. I was shy and always afraid of saying the wrong thing. Every new school, every new face, was a fresh start, but it also felt like a fresh wound. I'd look at the other kids, laughing and joking, and wonder what was wrong with me. Why couldn't I be like them? It was a lonely feeling, like being stranded on a deserted island.

The more alone I felt, the harder it became to connect with people. It was a vicious cycle. I was convinced that nobody wanted to be friends with me, so I pushed people away before they could push me away.

Dad's words, sharp like a knife, echoed in my head: "You don't belong anywhere." I was a puzzle piece that didn't fit anywhere.

One day, the silence was so loud I felt like I couldn't breathe. I was only six years old, but the world felt impossibly heavy. The constant change, the lack of stability, and the absence of love had built a wall around me, a wall that seemed to grow taller with each passing day. I felt so alone, so lost, like a tiny boat adrift in a stormy ocean.

That evening, the darkness inside me reached a point where I couldn't bear it any longer. Our house seemed to close in around me, wrapping me in a suffocating bubble. The thought of continuing to exist in that pain was unbearable. In a moment of desperation, I tried to end it all.

The details of what happened are hazy, like a dream so terrible you can't quite shake it. There was pain, confusion, and an overwhelming sense of finality. But then, there was also a flicker of something else - a tiny spark of life that refused to be extinguished.

I survived, but the experience left an indelible mark on me. It was a scar that ran deeper than any physical wound, a constant reminder of the darkness I had once inhabited. The child I was before that night was gone, replaced by a soul haunted by the fear of what could have been.

Chapter 4: Divorce and Its Impacts on a Child's Mind

"Children raised in extremely unhappy or violent intact homes face misery in childhood and tragic challenges in adulthood."

— Judith S. Wallerstein

The Fragility of Love

Children absorb their surroundings like sponges, thriving in peace and unraveling in chaos. When parents fight or separate, the emotional impact can shatter a child's sense of safety, much like a delicate glass sculpture breaking into countless pieces. The arguments, tension, and loss create fractures in a child's emotional foundation, leaving scars that often persist into adulthood. Just as a delicate glass sculpture can be shattered by a sudden impact, a child's sense of security and well-being can be fractured by the turmoil of their home life.

The impact of parental conflict on children is complex and varies depending on numerous factors, such as the age of the child, the severity of the conflict, and the presence of other supportive adults. However, it is clear that children can suffer greatly when their parents' relationship is troubled. They may experience a range of emotions including fear, anger, sadness, and confusion. These feelings can manifest in various ways, such as behavioral problems, academic difficulties, and physical symptoms. The long-term consequences of growing up in a chaotic home can be far-reaching. Children who experience chronic stress may have difficulty forming healthy relationships, regulating their emotions, and achieving their full potential.

For me, growing up in a home filled with constant tension and fear was like living in a never-ending storm. Love felt like a fragile thing that could disappear in an instant, replaced by anger and hurt. It was hard to trust anyone or believe in a safe world when the person who was supposed to protect me caused so much pain.

From a young age, I learned that the world wasn't a safe place. The volatility of my parents' relationship shaped my earliest perceptions of love and trust. The home, meant to be a sanctuary, felt more like a battlefield, a lesson that would influence how I viewed relationships and safety for years to come.

Later, I'd explore these feelings more deeply, understanding how they had molded my coping mechanisms and shaped my resilience. The emotional scars I carried weren't unique, but they were mine to heal. These experiences left deep scars, shaping how I viewed myself and the world around me. I didn't believe I was worthy of love because the people who were supposed to protect me had so often caused me pain. My self-worth became tied to the chaos around me, and it would take years to untangle those knots.

You know, when a child experiences this kind of environment, they start to believe that love and safety are fragile and conditional. For me, this meant that I couldn't rely on love to be a constant, comforting presence. Instead, it felt like love could vanish at any moment, just like the stability I so desperately needed. This belief followed me well into adulthood, influencing how I view the world and how I relate to others.

My father's relentless negativity and criticism made me feel worthless. I learned that no matter what I did, I could never meet his standards. This led me to internalize the belief that I wasn't good enough, that I didn't deserve love or respect.

This sense of unworthiness wasn't confined to my relationship with my father. It seeped into all my interactions. In friendships and romantic relationships, I often found myself expecting rejection or betrayal. If I believed I wasn't deserving of love, then it was almost a given that others would agree with me. This mindset made it incredibly difficult to trust people or to believe that anyone could genuinely care for me.

Growing up in this harsh environment also affected how I dealt with challenges and stress. The unpredictability of my home life made it hard to develop healthy coping mechanisms. Instead of learning how to handle problems in a constructive way, I often found myself overwhelmed by anxiety and depression. The weight of the past felt like a heavy burden that I couldn't escape.

This trauma often manifested in moments of intense fear and sadness. Simple problems could become monumental, and my emotional responses were frequently out of proportion to the situation. My ability to cope with everyday stressors was compromised, and I struggled to manage my feelings in a way that felt healthy or productive.

Eventually, when my parents decided to get divorced when I was only 2, the pain of this split entirely changed me. The world shattered into a million pieces, and small things felt huge. I couldn't handle life's ups and downs like other kids. It was like my world exploded when they stopped loving each other. I was too young to understand, and it scared me terribly.

It was a silent collapse, a slow-motion earthquake that left me buried beneath the rubble of confusion and fear. I was a child, my heart a tender bud, unprepared for the icy winds of their separation. The initial shock was a numbness, a blanketing of disbelief. How could the people who were supposed to be my safe harbor, my protectors, be caught in such a tempestuous storm? It was as if the sun had vanished, leaving me to navigate a world cloaked in perpetual twilight.

As I have previously shared, the physical separation from my mother was a gut-wrenching ordeal. It felt like a part of me had been forcibly removed. I clung to her, my tiny fingers digging into her clothes as if, by sheer force of will, I could prevent the inevitable. The memory of her face, etched with a mixture of sorrow and desperation, is a haunting image that has stayed with me through the years. At that moment, I felt utterly helpless, a pawn in a game I didn't understand. Abandonment, a word I wouldn't fully comprehend for years, cast its long shadow over my young mind.

The absence of my mother created a void that no one could fill. It was like living in a house with empty rooms, an echo chamber of silence and longing. Her laughter, her warmth, her comforting presence were all I craved. Instead, I was met with the harsh reality of a new family dynamic, one marked by tension and uncertainty.

My father's words often turned into sharp arrows that pierced my heart. His constant criticism of my mother painted her as a villain, a distorted image that conflicted with the loving mother I knew. I found myself caught in a tug-of-war between loyalty and love, a battle that left me exhausted and confused. The more he spoke ill of her, the more I retreated into myself, building walls to protect the image of my mother that I held dear.

I felt like a ghost in my own life, a silent observer of the chaos around me. The happiness and security I once knew had evaporated, replaced by a pervasive sense of unease. Simple joys were overshadowed by a constant undercurrent of worry and sadness. The world, once a place of wonder and excitement, became a battlefield where I struggled to survive.

The emotional turmoil I endured during those years left deep scars. I learned to suppress my feelings and to wear a mask of indifference to shield myself from further pain. Laughter became a forced performance, a way to hide the emptiness within. I carried the weight of the world on my small shoulders, a burden far too heavy for a child to bear.

The absence of maternal love, coupled with the harsh treatment from my father's girlfriends, created a toxic environment. I felt unloved, unwanted, and unworthy. The belief that I was inherently flawed took root, casting a long shadow over my self-esteem. I retreated into a world of fantasy, seeking solace in books and daydreams. The child I was before the divorce was a vibrant, curious soul filled with hope and optimism. I later became a mere shadow of that former self, a fragile spirit struggling to find its way in the darkness. The whispers of those early experiences would reverberate through the years, shaping the adult I would become.

The echoes of my parents' fights still ring in my ears, even though the house has been quiet for years. My dad's anger was a storm that could erupt at any moment, and Mom's silent tears were a constant reminder of the pain she endured.

My childhood was a blur of hiding, pretending not to see or hear, and wishing for a world beyond the four walls that felt like a prison. The laughter of other kids on sunny days seemed like a distant melody, a tune I couldn't quite reach.

The world outside my home seemed like a foreign land. I didn't know how to trust people, to let them in. Every kind gesture felt like a trap waiting to be revealed. I built walls around my heart, brick by brick, to protect myself from the pain I knew so well.

As I grew older, the cracks in my foundation started to show. I struggled with school, with friends, with the simple act of being a teenager. My self-esteem was shattered, like a mirror after a violent storm. I felt invisible like no one really saw me or cared if they did. I carried the weight of their pain, their anger, their love lost. It was a heavy burden for a young heart to bear. I tried to escape through distractions, through books, through music, but the darkness always found its way back in. My twenties were a blur of searching. I wandered through life, a lost soul, looking for a place to belong. Relationships were a minefield. I longed for closeness, for someone to really see me, but fear held me back.

The moment things started to feel real, I'd build a wall, pushing people away before they could hurt me. It was a lonely way to live. I'd construct these grand plans, these perfect pictures of my life. But they were like castles made of sand, crumbling at the slightest touch of reality. Every failure felt like a personal attack, confirming my deepest fears. I was a survivor, but I was also a prisoner of my own mind.

Building Resilience Amidst Chaos

It was a long, slow climb out of that dark place. There were days when hope felt like a distant star, impossible to reach. But with time and a lot of stumbling, I started to find my way back to myself. It wasn't until I started therapy that I began to understand the depth of the damage. The therapist was a gentle light in the darkness, helping me to piece together the broken parts of myself. Slowly, I started to see the patterns, the connections between my past and my present.

Rebuilding from such a past isn't easy, but therapy has been a crucial part of my journey. Therapy helped me confront the painful truths of my upbringing and work through the deep-seated insecurities that had taken root. It's been a process of learning to see myself as worthy of love and stability, even though those were things I struggled to believe I deserved.

Through therapy, I've started to understand how my early experiences shaped my beliefs and behaviors. This awareness has been the first step towards changing those old patterns. Rebuilding self-esteem means challenging the negative beliefs that were instilled in me and learning to value myself in a healthier, more positive way.

Healing is a long and winding road filled with setbacks and breakthroughs. Some days, the shadows of the past loom large, threatening to engulf me. But I am learning to live with them rather than be consumed by them. I am learning to trust myself, to believe in my worth, and to build healthy relationships.

Chapter 5: Understanding the Trauma

When I look back at my own childhood, the trauma I experienced during my parents' divorce is still palpable. It wasn't just about the arguments or the eventual separation; it was about the overwhelming sense of instability and confusion that came with it. I realize now how important it is to truly understand what a child goes through in such situations, not just from a clinical perspective but from a place of empathy and compassion.

As a child, I often felt like my emotions were overlooked. Adults around me seemed more focused on their own struggles, leaving little room to acknowledge mine. I remember feeling a deep sense of sadness and fear but also a kind of invisibility, as if my pain wasn't significant enough to be noticed.

This is why understanding the trauma of a child during a divorce is so crucial. It's about recognizing that their experiences are real and valid and that they need support just as much as anyone else involved.

For me, the chaos of my parents' relationship created a confusing world. The home, which should have been a place of safety and comfort, became a battleground. I felt like I was caught in the crossfire, struggling to understand why the people who were supposed to love and protect me were causing so much pain. It's vital to understand that this kind of turmoil can shatter a child's sense of security. The world becomes unpredictable, and trust becomes a fragile, elusive thing.

Understanding trauma means acknowledging its lingering effects on the mind and body. As I reflect on my childhood, I see how the turmoil shaped me. I didn't just lose my parents' marriage—I lost my sense of stability, trust, and safety. I learned to bottle up my feelings because I didn't know how to express them or who to turn to. The fear of making things worse, of adding to the tension, kept me silent. I still remember one particular night: the sound of my father's voice booming through the walls, my small hands pressing over my ears as I hid under the table. I thought if I stayed quiet enough, invisible enough, the storm would pass.

That silence followed me for years, creeping into my relationships and my sense of self. It took time and reflection to realize that my silence was a survival strategy but not one I had to carry forever. Children of divorce often carry invisible burdens. They might withdraw into themselves, act out, or seek control in small ways to make sense of the chaos. For me, it was perfectionism, an endless effort to be "good enough," as though my worth could somehow fix the brokenness around me.

Understanding the trauma a child experiences during a divorce also means acknowledging the wide range of emotions they may feel. For me, there was a mix of anger, sadness, confusion, and even guilt. I often wondered if I had done something wrong and if somehow I was to blame for the discord. These complex emotions can be overwhelming, and without proper guidance, a child can become lost in them.

Reflecting on my journey, I see the importance of providing children with a safe space to express themselves.

Whether through therapy, supportive conversations, or simply being there to listen without judgment, children need to know that their feelings are valid and important. This validation can be a powerful healing force, helping them to process their emotions and begin to heal.

In my case, it took years to unravel the tangled web of emotions and beliefs that had formed during those chaotic times. The trauma didn't just disappear; it lingered, influencing my relationships and self-worth well into adulthood. Understanding and addressing this trauma earlier could have made a significant difference in my life.

Understanding the trauma that children experience during a divorce isn't just an abstract concept—it's a deeply personal and necessary journey. It's about acknowledging their pain, giving them the tools to express their feelings, and providing the support they need to heal. By doing so, we can help them navigate through one of the most challenging experiences of their young lives with a little more grace and resilience.

How Children Cope with Divorce Trauma

Looking back on my own childhood, I can see the various ways I tried to cope with the emotional turmoil that came with my parents' divorce. Each child finds their own means of managing the stress and confusion, often without even realizing that they are doing so. These coping mechanisms are a way for children to protect themselves and make sense of a world that suddenly feels chaotic and unsafe.

One common way children cope is through withdrawal. I remember times when I would retreat into my own world, finding solace in books and daydreams. It was a form of escape, a way to create a safe space where the reality of my parents' conflicts couldn't reach me. This withdrawal can manifest in different ways—some children become quiet and introspective, while others may seem distant or disinterested in activities they once enjoyed. It's as if they are building an emotional wall to keep out the pain and confusion. Others might cope by seeking control over aspects of their lives where they feel powerless. For me, this meant becoming obsessively organized with my schoolwork and belongings. It was a small way to assert some sense of order amidst the chaos. Some children may develop perfectionist tendencies, believing that if they are "good enough," they can somehow fix the situation or prevent further conflicts. This coping strategy, while seemingly productive, often stems from a deep-seated need to regain a sense of stability and predictability.

Another way children might cope is by acting out. In my case, this wasn't as pronounced, but I've seen it in others who've gone through similar experiences. Some children might express their inner turmoil through rebellious behavior, aggression, or defiance. It's their way of voicing their frustration and confusion when they lack the words to articulate their feelings. Unfortunately, this behavior can often be misinterpreted by adults as mere disobedience rather than a cry for help.

Some children try to take on a caretaker role, attempting to mediate between parents or take care of siblings. This was something I often found myself doing—trying to soothe tensions, to be the "peacemaker." It's a way to feel useful and to alleviate some of the stress in the household. However, this role reversal can be harmful, as it places an enormous burden on the child, asking them to take on responsibilities far beyond their years. Another coping mechanism is the development of a "false self." To avoid further conflict or to please both parents, children might suppress their true feelings and adopt a persona they think will be more acceptable. I remember feeling like I had to be cheerful and agreeable, even when I was hurting inside. This false self can lead to a disconnection from their own emotions and a loss of authenticity.

Lastly, some children cope by seeking outside validation and approval. This often stems from a deep sense of insecurity and the need for reassurance. I found myself craving praise from teachers and other adults as a way to feel valued and seen. This can lead to a reliance on external validation for self-worth, which can be problematic later in life.

These coping mechanisms are not inherently "bad" or "good"; they are simply strategies that children use to navigate a challenging and often overwhelming situation. However, without proper support and understanding, these behaviors can become ingrained, leading to issues in adolescence and adulthood. It's essential for adults to recognize these signs and offer compassionate support, helping children process their emotions in healthier ways.

The Physical and Academic Impact of Divorce on Children

Moving on to the impacts of divorce. From my own experience and the stories of others, I've seen how a child's physical health and academic performance can be deeply affected by the upheaval of divorce.

When my parents divorced, it felt like my entire world was in disarray. This sense of instability didn't just affect my emotional state; it took a toll on my physical health. Stress and anxiety can manifest in physical symptoms, and I experienced this firsthand. My sleep patterns became irregular; I had trouble falling asleep and often woke up feeling exhausted. The constant worry and tension led to frequent headaches and stomachaches. It was as if my body was reflecting the turmoil my heart and mind were enduring.

Research supports that children going through a divorce are more susceptible to health problems. The stress of adjusting to new family dynamics, moving homes, or changing schools can weaken a child's immune system. They might catch colds more often or experience more severe illnesses. The emotional strain from the divorce exacerbates these issues, making children more vulnerable to both minor and more serious health concerns.

Academically, the effects of divorce are equally significant. I remember struggling to focus in school. The emotional distractions and the constant worry about my family situation made it difficult to concentrate on my studies. My grades began to slip, and I found it hard to stay engaged with my schoolwork. The transition of moving between two homes and adapting to new routines only added to the challenge. It felt like I was constantly juggling my feelings of confusion and sadness while trying to keep up with school. Children of divorced parents often show a decline in academic performance. The stress and distraction caused by their family situation can lead to difficulties in concentrating, a decline in motivation, and a decrease in academic achievement. The sudden changes in their home life can interrupt their focus and affect their ability to perform well in school.

Socially, the impact of divorce can be just as profound. Children may feel isolated and have trouble connecting with their peers. They might struggle to engage in social activities and may withdraw from friendships. This withdrawal is often a way to cope with the insecurity and confusion they feel. I recall feeling disconnected from my friends, unsure of how to relate to them or how to explain my family situation. This sense of isolation can further impact a child's emotional and social development.

Understanding these physical and academic impacts is crucial.

They highlight the need for a supportive environment that addresses not only the emotional aspects of divorce but also the practical challenges children face. Providing a stable routine, offering consistent support, and addressing health and educational needs can help mitigate these impacts.

The Importance of Communication over Enforcement

As we explore the wide-ranging impacts of divorce on children, it's essential to recognize that effective communication can be a powerful tool in helping them navigate this difficult transition. From my own experience and observations, I've seen how communication—or the lack thereof—can significantly affect a child's well-being during and after a divorce.

After my parents separated, there was a lot of decision-making about our living arrangements, schooling, and daily routines. While these decisions were necessary, what I needed most was not just the decisions themselves but the understanding and empathy behind them. Too often, the focus was on enforcing decisions rather than communicating openly with us about the changes. The lack of discussion about why things were happening made us feel like passive participants in our own lives. We needed to understand the reasons behind the decisions, to feel heard, and to be reassured that our feelings were valid.

When parents focus solely on enforcing decisions without engaging in meaningful communication, children can feel alienated and powerless. They may struggle to make sense of their new reality and may internalize feelings of frustration or confusion. In contrast, open dialogue helps children process their emotions and understand the reasons behind the changes. It gives them a sense of control and involvement in their own lives, even when the circumstances are beyond their control.

Communicating with children about the changes they are experiencing provides them with an opportunity to express their feelings and ask questions. It helps them feel supported and valued. For example, discussing how the divorce will affect their daily routines, explaining the reasons for changes in living arrangements, and reassuring them of your love and support can make a significant difference in their emotional adjustment.

During my own adjustment, I found that conversations with my parents, even when they were challenging, were crucial in helping me understand and accept the changes.

It was not just about being told what would happen next but about being listened to and having my concerns acknowledged. This open line of communication helped me process my emotions and made the transition less overwhelming.

Moreover, involving children in discussions about decisions that affect them helps build trust. It signals that their opinions and feelings matter, which can strengthen their emotional resilience. When children are given the opportunity to voice their thoughts and ask questions, they are more likely to feel supported and less likely to act out or internalize negative emotions. While enforcing decisions during a divorce is sometimes necessary, it is the quality of communication that can truly make a difference in a child's experience. By prioritizing open, honest conversations and actively listening to their concerns, parents can provide their children with the emotional support they need to navigate the challenges of divorce. It's not just about the decisions we make but how we involve our children in understanding and adapting to those decisions.

Chapter 6: Communicating with Your Child

A separation or a divorce is a highly stressful and emotional experience for everyone, but children feel it on a different level. Their worlds are turned upside down. It is traumatic, at any age, to witness your parents separating. It can leave a child feeling angry, shocked, and uncertain. Some kids may even feel guilty, blaming themselves for the problems at home.

One of the most challenging aspects of divorce is finding the right way to talk to your child about it. Children, depending on their age and maturity, can experience a wide range of emotions and concerns when their parents separate. How you communicate with them during this period can greatly influence their ability to cope and adapt to the new family structure.

It is absolutely paramount to know what to say and how to say it in a way that provides comfort, clarity, and support. Effective communication not only helps children process their feelings but also reassures them of their place in the family despite the changes. By approaching these difficult conversations with honesty, empathy, and sensitivity, you can help your child navigate this challenging transition with greater ease.

1. What to Say and How to Say It?

Talking to children about divorce is a challenge, but it's also an opportunity to create a foundation of trust and understanding. Children need to feel heard, valued, and reassured that the love of their parents remains constant, even as family dynamics change. By fostering open conversations, validating their feelings, and addressing their concerns honestly, parents can help their children navigate this transition with resilience. Each conversation, no matter how difficult, is a step toward healing and strengthening the bond you share.

Begin by being truthful with your child, but keep your explanations straightforward and age-appropriate. Children need to understand why the divorce is happening, but complex or lengthy explanations can be confusing and overwhelming. A simple statement such as "Mommy and Daddy have decided that we can't live together anymore" conveys the essential information without unnecessary detail.

The next step is to reassure your child. Your child needs to hear that your love for them has not changed. Reassure them that the divorce is not their fault and that both parents will continue to care for them. Phrases like, "I love you very much, and that won't ever change," can help alleviate feelings of insecurity. Reinforce that both parents are still there for them, even though they're going to be living separately. Moving on to acknowledging the changes is an equally important step as children often worry about what their new life will look like, so it's helpful to address the upcoming changes honestly and to provide them with some details about what to expect. For instance, explain where they will live, how often they will see each parent and any changes to their daily routines. This can help reduce anxiety by setting clear expectations.

While it's crucial to be honest, it's also important to avoid criticizing or blaming the other parent. Children are sensitive to negative comments about their parents and may feel caught in the middle. Instead, focus on what is happening and why without assigning fault. This approach helps to prevent your child from feeling as though they need to take sides or feel responsible for the breakup.

Whenever possible, discuss the divorce with your child together with your co-parent. This unified approach shows that both parents are on the same page and that the decision is not a result of one parent's actions alone. It also helps to reassure your child that both parents are committed to their well-being despite the separation.

Children may have many questions about the divorce. Be prepared to answer their queries honestly but gently. If you don't have all the answers, it's okay to admit it. Let your child know that you will address their concerns as best as you can and that you are there to support them through the process. Foster an environment where your child feels comfortable sharing their feelings. Let them know that it's okay to express their emotions and ask questions. Regular, open conversations about the divorce can help them process their feelings and understand that their emotions are valid and expected. The conversation about divorce shouldn't be a one-time event. As your child grows and their understanding evolves, they may have new questions or concerns. Be open to revisiting the topic and continue providing reassurance and support as they adjust to the changes.

Throughout your conversations, show empathy and patience. Divorce is a challenging time for children, and your supportive and understanding approach can significantly impact their emotional adjustment. By providing consistent, caring communication, you can help your child navigate this difficult transition with greater resilience and confidence.

2. Listen to Them, and Be Honest About Your Feelings

Communication is a two-way street, and when it comes to discussing divorce with your child, it's crucial to not only share your thoughts but also to listen to theirs. Children may struggle to articulate their emotions during this time, and as a parent, your role is to provide a safe space for them to express themselves.

Begin by asking open-ended questions like, "How are you feeling about everything?" or "Is there anything you want to talk about?" These questions encourage your child to share their thoughts and feelings without feeling pressured to give a specific response. When they do speak, give them your full attention. Put aside any distractions, maintain eye contact, and listen without interrupting. Your child needs to feel heard and understood, and your attentiveness will convey that their feelings are valid and important.

Being honest about your own emotions is just as important. Children are often more perceptive than we realize, and they can sense when something is wrong, even if it isn't openly discussed. By sharing your feelings in an age-appropriate way, you model healthy emotional expression. For example, you might say, "I'm feeling sad about the changes in our family, but I know we'll get through this together." This honesty helps your child understand that it's okay to have complex emotions and that they are not alone in their feelings.

However, while it's important to be open, be mindful not to burden your child with too much information or to share details that might be overwhelming or confusing. The goal is to be transparent while still protecting them from unnecessary stress. Keep your explanations simple, and reassure them that it's normal to have mixed feelings during such a significant change.

3. Acknowledge Their Feelings and Let Them Know That It's Not Their Fault

One of the most common concerns children have during a divorce is the fear that they are somehow to blame for the separation. This fear can manifest in many ways; it can be through guilt, anxiety, or even acting out. As a parent, it's essential to address this concern head-on and reassure your child that the divorce is not their fault.

When your child expresses their feelings, whether it's anger, sadness, or confusion, acknowledge those emotions without judgment. You might say, "I can see that you're feeling really upset right now, and that's okay. It's a big change, and it's natural to feel a lot of different things." Validating their feelings helps them feel understood and supported, which is critical for their emotional well-being.

Next, clearly communicate that the decision to divorce was made by the adults and that it had nothing to do with anything they did or didn't do. This might be something you need to repeat multiple times in different conversations, as children often need reassurance on this point. You could say something like, "I want you to know that this decision wasn't because of anything you did. Sometimes grown-ups have problems that they can't solve together, and that's what happened here."

By consistently acknowledging their feelings and dispelling any notion of blame, you help your child develop a healthier perspective on the situation. This understanding allows them to focus on adapting to the new family dynamics without carrying the unnecessary burden of guilt.

4. Give Reassurance and Love

During a divorce, children need constant reassurance and expressions of love from their parents. The uncertainty and changes that come with divorce can make them feel insecure and anxious about their place in the family. Your consistent reassurance and love are vital in helping them through this challenging time.

Start by regularly affirming your love for your child. Simple phrases like "I love you," "I'm here for you," and "You are very important to me" can go a long way in providing emotional security. Make an effort to say these things frequently, especially during moments when your child seems particularly vulnerable or upset.

Physical affection is also important. Hugs, a pat on the back, or just sitting close together can provide a sense of comfort and safety. Physical touch can be incredibly soothing and can reinforce your verbal expressions of love and support.

In addition to words and physical affection, show your love through actions. Spend quality time together doing activities your child enjoys. Whether it's playing a game, reading a book, or simply talking, these moments reinforce your bond and provide a sense of normalcy and joy amidst the changes.

It's also necessary to have patience and to be understanding. Children express their emotions in various ways; they may act out or completely withdraw. Respond to these behaviors with empathy and support rather than frustration. Let your kids know that it's okay to feel sad, angry, or confused, and you're there to help them through it.

5. Provide Comfort and Stability Through the Divorce

Providing comfort and stability can go a long way to help your child cope with the upheaval of divorce. Children thrive on routine and predictability, which can be disrupted during a separation. Maintaining stability as much as possible helps children feel secure and supported.

One of the most effective ways to provide stability is by keeping daily routines consistent. Regular meal times, bedtimes, and other daily activities should be maintained as much as possible. This consistency provides a sense of regularity and helps children know what to expect, which can be very comforting during times of change. If there are changes to routines, such as different living arrangements or visitation schedules, explain these changes clearly and calmly to your child. Provide a visual schedule if it helps them understand and anticipate what's coming next. Knowing what to expect helps your child feel more in control.

Comfort also comes from a stable and supportive home environment. Make your home a safe haven where your child can relax and feel secure. Create a calm and loving atmosphere by managing your own stress and emotions. Children often take cues from their parents, so demonstrating calmness and resilience can help them feel more at ease.

It's also important to encourage your child to engage in familiar and comforting activities. Whether it's playing with friends, participating in extracurricular activities, or spending time on hobbies they enjoy, these activities can provide a sense of continuity and joy.

Finally, seek additional support if needed. Counseling or therapy can be beneficial for children struggling to cope with divorce. A professional can provide a safe space for your child to express their feelings and develop coping strategies. Don't hesitate to seek help for yourself as well, as your well-being directly impacts your ability to support your child.

Divorce is tough on everyone, especially kids. Talking openly, listening carefully, and letting your child know you love them can make a big difference. Be there for them, keep things as normal as possible, and remember that your love is the most important thing. With time and care, you can help your child heal and grow stronger.

Chapter 7: Helping Your Child Cope

Divorce is a life-altering event that can shake the foundation of a family. Divorce often leaves children feeling lost, confused, and scared. While it's impossible to shield children entirely from the pain of their parent's separation, the way parents traverse this challenging time can considerably impact their child's emotional well-being and long-term development.

The purpose of this chapter is to offer practical guidance to help parents support their children through the divorce process. By understanding the emotional turmoil children may experience and implementing effective coping strategies, parents can create a nurturing environment that creates resilience and growth within their children. Ultimately, the goal is to equip children with the tools they need to navigate this challenging chapter of their lives and emerge stronger on the other side.

Encourage Open Communication

Helping your child cope goes beyond just conversations; it's about creating an environment where they feel safe to express their feelings over time. I remember the small gestures that made a difference for me as a child: a teacher who let me stay in the classroom during recess when I felt overwhelmed or a neighbor who invited me to help bake cookies. Those moments reminded me I wasn't entirely alone, even when life felt unbearable.

As a parent, these small acts of reassurance, a hug, a consistent routine, or simply sitting quietly with your child can speak volumes. Coping isn't a one-time fix; it's a gradual process of building trust and stability.

Understand Individual Responses

Children of different ages and personalities will process the divorce in unique ways. While some may openly discuss their feelings, others might act out or withdraw. Pay close attention to your child's behavior and emotional cues, and be flexible in your approach. What works for one child might not work for another, so be prepared to adapt your strategies to meet their individual needs.

Minimize Conflict

If possible, try to minimize conflict between you and your ex-partner, as constant disputes can create a tense environment for your child. When parents argue in front of their children, it can lead to feelings of confusion and divided loyalty. Strive to maintain a respectful and cooperative relationship with your ex, keeping disagreements away from your child's view. This helps prevent your child from feeling caught in the middle and supports their emotional well-being.

Seek Help When Needed

Don't hesitate to reach out for help if you need it. This could be support from family and friends or professional assistance if your child shows signs of distress. Consult your child's pediatrician or a mental health professional if you notice persistent behavioral issues or emotional struggles. Professional guidance can provide additional tools and strategies to support both you and your child during this challenging time.

Be Kind to Yourself

As you navigate the complexities of divorce, remember to be kind to yourself. It's natural to experience a range of emotions, and it's okay to show vulnerability in front of your children. Your emotional openness can help them feel more comfortable sharing their own feelings. Taking care of your own mental health will better equip you to support your child.

The effects of divorce on children can vary, but research shows that they are generally resilient. The first few years may be particularly challenging, but many children eventually adapt and thrive. In some cases, children living in high-conflict environments may even see the separation as a positive change.

Co-Parenting Effectively: Avoiding the Pitfalls of Conflict

Effective co-parenting is crucial in helping your child manage the emotional terrain of divorce. When parents work together, even after separation, they create a stable environment that can greatly reduce the stress and anxiety their child might feel. However, when co-parenting is marred by conflict, blame, or communication breakdowns, it can have a detrimental impact on your child's emotional well-being.

The Role of Co-Parenting in a Child's Well-Being

Children often look to their parents for cues on how to react and feel during challenging times. When parents are able to communicate respectfully and cooperate in parenting duties, it sends a message of stability and unity to the child, even if the family dynamic has changed. Co-parenting effectively means maintaining a partnership focused on your child's best interests, regardless of personal differences.

Effective co-parenting involves:

1. **Consistent Communication**: Keep an open line of communication with your ex-partner about your child's needs, activities, and any issues that arise. This ensures that both parents are on the same page and can respond to their child's needs in a consistent manner.

2. **Unified Decision-Making**: When parents make decisions together about their child's education, health, and extracurricular activities, it prevents confusion and gives the child a sense of security. It's important to present a united front so the child knows that both parents are involved and invested in their well-being.

3. **Respect and Courtesy**: Treat your ex-partner with respect, especially in front of your child. Even if there are unresolved issues between you, keeping interactions polite and professional helps create a calm and reassuring atmosphere for your child.

Avoiding the Trap of Putting Your Child in the Middle

One of the most harmful things parents can do during and after a divorce is to put their child in the middle of their conflicts. This can take many forms, such as:

- **Using the Child as a Messenger**: Asking your child to relay messages between you and your ex-partner puts them in an uncomfortable position. It can lead to misunderstandings and make the child feel responsible for the communication between their parents.

- **Blaming the Child for the Divorce**: It's crucial that your child understands they are not to be blamed for the divorce. Children might internalize conflict and believe that their actions or behavior contributed to the separation. Make it clear that the decision to divorce was an adult decision, and nothing they did caused it.

- **Speaking Negatively About the Other Parent**: Badmouthing your ex-partner in front of your child forces them to take sides, which can lead to feelings of guilt, confusion, and loyalty conflicts. This can severely damage the child's relationship with one or both parents.

The Importance of Keeping the Focus on Your Child

By keeping your child out of the middle of adult conflicts, you protect their emotional health and allow them to process the divorce in a healthier way. It's important to always keep the focus on your child's needs, feelings, and well-being rather than letting personal grievances interfere with your parenting.

When you co-parent effectively, you provide a strong foundation for your child to build upon as they adapt to their new circumstances. Remember, your child is navigating this transition alongside you. By maintaining a respectful and cooperative co-parenting relationship, you help ease their journey and provide the stability they need to thrive.

Seeking Professional Help: When to Involve a Therapist or Counselor

Divorce is a significant life event that can be overwhelming for children, regardless of their age. While parents can provide essential support, there may be times when the challenges are too complex for a family to handle alone. In such cases, seeking professional help from a therapist or counselor can be an invaluable step in ensuring your child's emotional well-being.

Recognizing When Your Child Needs Professional Support

It's not always easy to recognize when your child might need professional help, especially during a time of upheaval like divorce. Children often struggle with expressing their feelings, and their distress can manifest in various ways. Signs that your child might benefit from therapy include persistent sadness or anxiety, noticeable behavioral changes, or physical symptoms like frequent headaches or stomachaches. Additionally, if your child has difficulty adjusting to new routines or expresses feelings of hopelessness or despair, these are clear indications that professional intervention is needed.

The Role of a Therapist or Counselor

A therapist or counselor provides a safe and neutral space where your child can express their feelings without fear of judgment. They are trained to help children process complex emotions, develop coping strategies, and work through the unique challenges that arise during a divorce. Professional support can be especially beneficial because therapists offer an objective perspective, use specialized techniques tailored to children, and provide guidance to parents, ensuring that the entire family is working together to create a healthy environment.

How to Approach the Idea of Therapy with Your Child

Introducing the idea of therapy to your child requires sensitivity and care. It's important to emphasize that seeking help is a positive step toward feeling better. You can explain that talking to someone who understands feelings, like a counselor, can be helpful, especially when dealing with big changes like divorce. Reassure your child that therapy is a safe place where they can talk about anything on their mind and that it's okay to have mixed feelings about the situation.

Finding the Right Professional

When seeking professional help, it's crucial to find a therapist or counselor who specializes in working with children and has experience dealing with divorce-related issues. You can start by asking your pediatrician for a recommendation or seeking referrals from other parents who have gone through similar experiences. Involving your child in the process, allowing them to meet potential therapists and choose someone they feel comfortable with, is essential for the success of the therapy.

The Benefits of Professional Help

Involving a professional can make a significant difference in your child's ability to cope with the divorce. Therapy provides your child with the tools they need to understand and manage their emotions, fostering resilience and emotional intelligence that will benefit them throughout their lives. Seeking professional help is an investment in your child's future, showing them that their feelings matter and that it's okay to ask for help when life gets tough. With the right support, your child can emerge from this challenging time with greater emotional strength and a healthier outlook on the changes in their life.

Helping your child cope with the emotional challenges of divorce requires a delicate balance of communication, understanding, and support. By engaging in honest conversations, actively listening, and acknowledging their feelings, you can create an environment where your child feels safe and valued. Co-parenting effectively and avoiding putting your child in the middle of conflicts helps to minimize additional stress and confusion. When needed, seeking professional help can provide your child with the resources to navigate their emotions and build resilience. The key takeaway is that, with empathy and patience, you can guide your child through this transition, ensuring they feel secure and loved, regardless of how the family structure changes.

Chapter 8: How Can You Cope?

When parents separate, the pain and confusion that children endure can be overwhelming, especially when the relationship between those parents is violent or abusive. For a child witnessing such trauma, the emotional scars can run deep, leaving them with a fractured sense of security and a skewed understanding of relationships. The impact of this environment often lingers long after the separation, shaping how they view themselves and their interactions with others.

In the midst of this turmoil, it's important to remember that healing is possible. Coping with the aftermath of a violent parental relationship requires time, patience, and a willingness to confront difficult emotions. For children who have lived through such experiences, acknowledging the trauma is the first step. It's okay to feel hurt, scared, or even angry about what has happened. These feelings are natural responses to a situation that no child should ever have to endure.

But as painful as it may be, understanding that the violence was not their fault is crucial. Children often internalize their parents' conflicts, believing that if they had just been better, quieter, or more obedient, the violence would have stopped. This is a heavy burden for any child to carry, and it's essential to release this self-blame and recognize that the responsibility for the violence lies solely with the parents. When I was young, I found myself caught in the crossfire of my parents' toxic relationship. The constant tension, the fights, and the emotional volatility left me feeling lost and afraid. For a long time, I didn't know how to make sense of the chaos around me, and I certainly didn't know how to cope with the emptiness it left inside me when they finally separated.

As I grew older, I realized that the void I felt wasn't just from the physical absence of one parent or the other – it was from the loss of the family unit I had known, flawed as it was. The security that I had associated with having both parents in my life, however imperfectly, was gone, and I had to learn how to navigate life without it.

One of the ways I began to cope with this gap in my life was by allowing myself to grieve. Grieving wasn't just about mourning the loss of my parent's marriage; it was about accepting that my childhood was different from what I had hoped it would be. It was about coming to terms with the fact that my family, as I had known it, could no longer be the same.

I also found solace in talking to others who had been through similar experiences. Sharing my story, listening to theirs, and realizing that I wasn't alone helped me process my feelings in a way that I couldn't do on my own. There is strength in community, and sometimes, the most healing thing we can do is reach out to others who understand our pain. As I began to rebuild my life, I discovered that filling the gaps left by my parents' divorce meant creating new sources of stability and love. I focused on nurturing relationships with friends, mentors, and eventually my own family. These connections didn't replace what I had lost, but they did provide me with a sense of belonging and support that I had desperately needed.

Coping with the aftermath of a hostile family environment is not easy, and the journey is different for everyone. But by acknowledging the pain, seeking support, and gradually rebuilding your sense of self, it is possible to heal and find peace. The process may be slow, and setbacks are inevitable, but each step forward is a testament to your resilience and strength.

Dealing with Your Feelings

The journey of coping with the trauma of an abusive parental relationship begins with confronting and processing your feelings. It might seem easier to bury your emotions, pretending that everything is okay or that the past doesn't affect you. However, unresolved feelings can fester, leading to more significant issues down the road. It's essential to give yourself permission to feel the pain, sadness, anger, and confusion that come with your experience. These emotions are valid, and acknowledging them is the first step toward healing. Talking about what you're going through with someone you trust can be incredibly liberating. Whether it's a close friend, a family member, or a counselor, sharing your thoughts and feelings helps to unburden your mind. This process not only provides relief but also helps you gain perspective on your situation. Sometimes, just hearing yourself talk out loud can bring clarity and understanding that might not come from internalizing your emotions.

Surrounding Yourself with Trustworthy People

During times of emotional turmoil, the people you surround yourself with play a critical role in your healing process. Trust is key. It's important to build a support network of individuals who genuinely care about you and have your interests at heart. These are the people who will offer a listening ear, sound advice, and a safe space for you to express yourself without judgment.

Having a reliable support system can make a significant difference in how you cope with your situation. These are the people who can provide comfort during the tough times and celebrate your progress as you move forward. They can also help you maintain a sense of normalcy and stability when everything else seems uncertain.

Avoiding Unhealthy Coping Outlets

When faced with overwhelming emotions, it can be tempting to seek out quick fixes or distractions to numb the pain. Unfortunately, turning to unhealthy coping mechanisms like drugs, alcohol, or bad company can lead one to a downward spiral that only exacerbates your problem. These outlets may provide temporary relief, but they come with long-term consequences that can be far more damaging than the original pain you were trying to escape.

Instead of falling into these traps, it's crucial to find healthier ways to cope with your emotions. This might include engaging in physical activities, pursuing hobbies, or practicing mindfulness and meditation. These alternatives can help you manage stress and anxiety without the negative side effects associated with unhealthy behaviors.

Joining Support Groups

One of the most powerful ways to cope with the effects of a volatile home environment is by connecting with others who have gone through similar experiences. Support groups can offer a sense of belonging and understanding that is often hard to find elsewhere. In these groups, you can share your story and listen to others, finding comfort in the knowledge that you are not alone.

Being part of a support group allows you to learn from others who have been in your shoes. You can gain valuable insights into different coping strategies, hear stories of resilience and recovery, and receive encouragement from people who truly understand what you're going through. This shared experience can be incredibly healing and can help you feel more empowered to face your own challenges.

Expressing Your Feelings Instead of Suppressing Them

Suppressing emotions might seem like a way to protect yourself from further pain, but in reality, it only prolongs your suffering. When you bottle up your feelings, they don't go away – they linger and can resurface in unhealthy ways. It's essential to find healthy outlets for expressing your emotions.

This might mean talking to someone you trust, writing in a journal, creating art, or even just crying when you need to. Expressing your feelings can be cathartic and helps you process what you're going through. It's a way to release the emotional pressure that builds up inside, allowing you to move forward with a clearer mind and a lighter heart. Coping with the aftermath of a divorce is a challenging journey, but by dealing with your feelings, surrounding yourself with trustworthy people, avoiding unhealthy outlets, joining support groups, and expressing your emotions, you can begin to heal and rebuild your life.

Moving on and Embracing Change

Moving on from the trauma of a violent parental relationship is a comprehensive process that involves both personal growth and adaptation. For many, the journey starts with acknowledging the past and understanding its impact on your present and future. It's essential to recognize that moving on doesn't mean forgetting or dismissing your experiences; rather, it involves finding ways to integrate those experiences into a narrative that allows you to move forward with resilience and hope.

1. Embrace Self-Compassion: One of the first steps in moving on is practicing self-compassion. Recognize that healing is a gradual process and that it's okay to have setbacks along the way. Be kind to yourself, and understand that your journey is unique. Treat yourself with the same empathy and support that you would offer to a friend in a similar situation.

2. Set Personal Goals: Moving on often involves setting new goals and envisioning a future that goes beyond the trauma. Focus on what you want to achieve personally, professionally, and emotionally. Setting goals gives you direction and a sense of purpose, helping you build a future that aligns with your values and aspirations.

3. Build New Routines: Establishing new routines and habits can be incredibly grounding. Routines provide structure and stability, which are crucial when adjusting to changes in your life. Whether it's adopting a new hobby, starting a new job, or simply incorporating regular self-care practices into your daily life, new routines can help you feel more in control and positive about the future.

4. Seek Professional Guidance: Professional help can be invaluable in the process of moving on. Therapy or counseling provides a safe space to explore your feelings, gain insights, and develop coping strategies. A mental health professional can guide you through the process of healing, helping you to address unresolved issues and move forward with confidence.

5. Foster Positive Relationships: Surround yourself with people who uplift and support you. Positive relationships are crucial for emotional well-being and can provide a network of encouragement as you navigate your new path. Engage with friends, family, or community groups that foster a supportive environment.

6. Practice Resilience: Resilience is the ability to bounce back from adversity and adapt to change. Cultivating resilience involves building coping skills, maintaining a hopeful outlook, and learning to manage stress effectively. Practicing mindfulness, engaging in physical activity, and maintaining a balanced lifestyle are all ways to enhance your resilience.

Adjusting to change is essential for several reasons. Firstly, it allows you to adapt to new circumstances and opportunities with a positive attitude. Change is an inevitable part of life, and how you respond to it can significantly impact your overall well-being and happiness. Embracing change helps you to grow, learn, and develop a greater sense of self-efficacy.

Coping with divorce is a process that requires patience and self-care. For me, it started with finding moments of peace in unexpected places, like writing in a journal or walking around my neighborhood. I didn't have all the answers, and I still don't, but those small rituals helped me feel grounded when everything else seemed uncertain.

One memory stands out: sitting by the window during a storm, watching the rain streak down the glass. At that moment, I let myself feel the sadness fully, without judgment. It was one of the first steps toward acknowledging my pain and finding ways to move forward. Moreover, adjusting to change encourages flexibility and adaptability. These qualities are crucial in navigating the uncertainties of life and seizing new opportunities. By learning to embrace and manage change, you develop a more robust capacity to handle future challenges and transitions.

In summary, moving on from past trauma involves a combination of self-compassion, goal-setting, routine-building, professional guidance, fostering positive relationships, and practicing resilience. Embracing change is a crucial part of this process, enabling you to adapt, grow, and build a fulfilling future. As you move forward, remember that healing is a journey, and each step you take brings you closer to a more balanced and hopeful life.

Chapter 9: The Bright Side

It's easy to get caught up in feelings of loss, anger, and sadness when dealing with the aftermath of a parental divorce. These emotions are natural, but they can often overshadow the positives in your life. The journey of coping with your parents' divorce is not just about managing these negative emotions; it's also about shifting your focus and living in the present. By doing so, you can find a path forward that is not defined by past pain but by the possibilities that lie ahead.

To help cope with the aftermath of a parental divorce, it's important to understand the psychological effects of grief and trauma that can arise from such a significant life change. Grief, often associated with the loss of a loved one, can also occur in response to the end of a marriage. The emotional response can vary widely, ranging from mild sadness to deep despair. It's not uncommon to experience a range of emotions, including guilt, anger, fear, and confusion, as you navigate this challenging period.

Short-Term Impacts of Grief During Divorce

Grief can have immediate effects on your mental health and cognitive function. You may notice difficulty focusing, impaired memory, or even challenges in making sound judgments. These effects stem from the parts of the brain responsible for learning and memory, which can be significantly impacted during times of intense emotional stress.

Understanding Trauma and Its Connection to Divorce

Trauma is defined as an experience that causes intense fear, helplessness, or horror. Like grief, trauma can have a profound impact on mental health and well-being. Divorce, especially if it involves betrayal, abuse, or other intense conflicts, can be a traumatic experience. Symptoms such as intrusive memories, nightmares, flashbacks, depression, and anxiety may manifest as a result.

Divorce and PTSD

While Post-Traumatic Stress Disorder (PTSD) is often associated with severe traumas like accidents or natural disasters, the stress from a high-conflict divorce can also trigger PTSD. This condition is characterized by the hyperarousal of the body's stress response system and long-term emotional disturbances. The persistent stress of a contentious divorce can take a toll on your mental health, potentially leading to disorders like depression and anxiety.

The Difficulty of Moving On

Why is it so challenging to move on after a divorce? The same parts of the brain affected by grief and trauma also play a role in forming associations between people, places, and experiences. These associations can become deeply ingrained, making it difficult to break unhealthy patterns and truly move on from the past.

Focusing on the Present

Living in the present is crucial when dealing with the trauma of divorce. It's common for children and even adults to dwell on what life was like before the separation or worry incessantly about the future. These thoughts can be overwhelming and lead to unnecessary stress. However, when you focus on the present moment, you can start to appreciate the things that are going right in your life.

One effective way to live in the moment is by paying attention to your surroundings. Whether you're at home, at school, or with friends, take a moment to notice what's around you. The colors, the sounds, the smells—these small details can help ground you in the present. By anchoring yourself in the here and now, you can prevent your mind from wandering to negative thoughts about the past or fears about the future.

For instance, if you find yourself feeling overwhelmed by the changes at home, try to focus on something positive in your immediate environment. This could be the warmth of the sun on your face, the sound of birds outside your window, or the laughter of a friend. These small, positive moments can serve as reminders that not everything has changed and that there are still good things in your life.

The Power of Mindfulness

Mindfulness and gratitude can transform your outlook, helping you focus on the present rather than dwelling on past pain. For me, this transformation began in the smallest of ways: learning to breathe through a moment of panic or noticing the warmth of sunlight on my face. At first, it felt insignificant; how could such simple acts counterbalance years of pain?

But over time, these moments became anchors, pulling me back to the present when my thoughts threatened to spiral. Gratitude, too, began as a reluctant practice. Writing one thing I was thankful for each day felt like a chore until I realized it was reshaping how I saw the world. The more I looked for beauty, the more I found it.

Mindfulness can be especially helpful when you're dealing with difficult emotions. For example, if you find yourself feeling sad or angry about your parents' divorce, mindfulness allows you to acknowledge these feelings without letting them control you. You might say to yourself, "I'm feeling sad right now, and that's okay." By accepting your emotions without any judgment, you can prevent them from overwhelming you.

You can practice mindfulness through activities like meditation, deep breathing, or even just going on a quiet walk. The key is to stay focused on the present moment and to let go of any thoughts or worries that are pulling you away from it.

Gratitude and Acceptance

Another important aspect of focusing on the positives is practicing gratitude. It's easy to overlook the good things in your life when you're dealing with a major upheaval like a parental divorce. However, taking the time to acknowledge what you're grateful for can have a profound impact on your mental well-being.

You might start by making a list of things you're thankful for each day. These could be big things, like the support of a close friend, or small things, like a favorite meal or a beautiful sunset. By regularly reflecting on the positive aspects of your life, you can begin to shift your focus away from what you've lost and toward what you still have.

Acceptance also plays a key role in finding the bright side after a divorce. This doesn't mean that you have to like or agree with everything that's happening, but it does mean acknowledging that some things are beyond your control. By accepting the situation as it is, rather than wishing it were different, you can begin to move forward and make the best of your current circumstances.

Building Positive Relationships

The people you choose to be around can have a significant impact on your ability to stay positive and present. After a divorce, it's important to seek out relationships that are supportive and uplifting. Whether it's friends, family members, or a trusted adult like a teacher or counselor, having a strong support system can make all the difference.

These relationships provide a safe space where you can express your feelings and receive the encouragement you need to keep moving forward. Positive social support can also help you stay grounded in the present, as the people around you remind you of the good things in your life.

On the flip side, it's important to be mindful of relationships that might be dragging you down. If there are people in your life who are constantly negative or who encourage you to dwell on the past, it might be time to distance yourself from them. Instead, focus on building connections with those who inspire you to be your best self and who help you see the positives in every situation.

Embracing Change

One of the most challenging aspects of dealing with a parental divorce is accepting the changes that come with it. Life as you knew it has been altered, and it can be difficult to adjust to this new reality. However, change is an inevitable part of life, and learning to embrace it can open up new opportunities for growth and happiness.

Instead of resisting change, try to view it as a chance to start fresh. This might mean developing new routines, finding new hobbies, or even redefining your relationship with your parents. By embracing the changes in your life, you can begin to see them as opportunities rather than obstacles.

For example, if you're now splitting your time between two homes, try to find something positive about each place. Maybe one parent lives closer to your school, making it easier to see friends, or perhaps the other has a pet that you love spending time with. By focusing on the positives in each situation, you can begin to adjust to the changes in your life with a more open and optimistic mindset.

Moving Forward with Hope

Ultimately, finding the bright side after a parental divorce is about moving forward with hope. It's about acknowledging the pain and difficulties you've faced but choosing not to let them define your future. Instead, you focus on the positives in your life, live in the present moment, and embrace the changes that come your way.

This doesn't mean that everything will be perfect or that you won't have bad days. But by making a conscious effort to stay positive and present, you can build a life that is not defined by your parents' divorce but by the strength, resilience, and hope that you carry within you.

Moving forward also involves setting goals for yourself and working toward them. Whether it's excelling in school, pursuing a hobby, or building stronger relationships, having something to strive for can help you stay focused on the future rather than dwelling on the past.

Remember, you are not alone in this journey. Many people have faced similar challenges and have come out stronger on the other side. By staying positive, focusing on the present, and embracing the changes in your life, you, too, can find the bright side and create a future filled with hope and possibility.

Understanding Your Feelings and Your Parents' Feelings

After a divorce, your emotions can be overwhelming, ranging from sadness and anger to confusion. It's vital to recognize that these feelings are a natural part of coping with major change. Acknowledging your emotions is the first step toward healing, even when it feels impossible.

At the same time, it's essential to understand that your parents are experiencing their own emotions and challenges. They, too, are dealing with pain, regrets, and uncertainties about the future. While it might be hard to see beyond your own feelings, recognizing that your parents are also struggling can help you understand their actions and decisions.

Your parents' pursuit of happiness doesn't mean they are disregarding your feelings. Their choices, though they might seem confusing or hurtful, often come from a desire to find peace and stability for themselves and for you. Understanding their perspective doesn't invalidate your emotions but adds depth to the shared experience of your family's transition.

It's crucial to realize that your parents' happiness and yours are not in opposition. Their efforts to create a new life for themselves might eventually lead to a better situation for everyone, even if it's hard to see that now. This understanding can help you move past resentment and open up to the possibility of a more peaceful future. As you work through your emotions, allow yourself to consider that your parents' journey could lead to positive changes for your family. Understanding their feelings, along with your own, is a key part of the healing process. By doing so, you create the potential for everyone to find a new sense of harmony, even after the difficulties of divorce.

My healing journey taught me the value of mindfulness. It started with small acts, a moment of quiet gratitude, the warmth of sunlight on my face, that anchored me to the present. Over time, these practices became my lifeline, showing me that even amidst the shadows, there is light.

Chapter 10: Healing from It All

Divorce, by its nature, is a deeply emotional and often painful process. It can leave lasting wounds that, if left unhealed, can continue to affect your life long after the final papers are signed. The feelings of betrayal, hurt, and anger that arise from a divorce are real and valid, but holding onto them can trap you in a cycle of pain and resentment. In this final chapter, let's explore the powerful concept of forgiveness and the importance of letting go, not just for the sake of your relationships but for your own peace of mind and future happiness.

The Weight of Unforgiveness

When trust is broken and hearts are wounded, it's natural to feel anger and sadness. But when these feelings linger, they can begin to overshadow every aspect of your life. Unforgiveness and holding onto resentment are like carrying a heavy burden; they weigh you down, keep you stuck in the past, and prevent you from moving forward. The pain of divorce, if not addressed, can manifest in many ways: strained relationships, difficulty trusting others, reluctance to embrace new opportunities, and even physical and mental health issues. It can make you reluctant to open up to others and rob you of the joy and beauty that life has to offer.

The Path to Forgiveness

Forgiveness is not about forgetting or excusing the past—it's about choosing freedom over the weight of resentment. I used to think forgiveness meant letting the people who hurt me off the hook, but I've learned that it's really about letting myself off the hook. It's about releasing the grip that anger and pain have on my life.

For a long time, I carried the burden of my father's actions. His words and deeds were like chains, binding me to a past I couldn't change. But forgiveness didn't come all at once—it came in pieces, as I began to understand that holding onto anger only kept me tethered to the pain.

The hardest part was seeing my parents as more than just their mistakes. Through therapy and reflection, I began to understand their struggles and their humanity. They were flawed people trying to navigate their own pain, and while their actions left scars, they didn't define my worth. Forgiveness has been the most liberating gift I've given myself. It doesn't mean I've forgotten or condoned what happened, but it means I've chosen to live without the weight of bitterness.

1. Commit to Letting Go

Forgiveness is not something that happens overnight. It's a process that requires time, reflection, and a deep commitment to change. Recognize that holding onto pain is only hurting you, and make the decision to let go. This commitment is the first and most crucial step toward healing.

2. Reflect on the Impact of Unforgiveness

Consider how holding onto negative emotions is affecting your life. Is it straining your relationships with others? Is it making you unhappy or preventing you from moving forward? Reflect on these questions and recognize the ways in which unforgiveness is holding you back. Then, think about the benefits of forgiveness—how it can free you from the past, bring peace into your life, and open the door to new possibilities.

3. Recognize Your Power of Choice

You cannot control what others do, but you have complete control over your actions and thoughts. You can choose to stop reliving the hurt and instead focus on the present and future. This realization is empowering because it means you have the ability to change your mindset and, in doing so, change your life.

4. Empathize with Your Parents

One of the most challenging aspects of forgiveness is seeing the situation from the other person's perspective. Try to understand why they may have acted the way they did. What circumstances, emotions, or past experiences could have influenced their behavior? This doesn't mean excusing their actions but rather understanding them, which can make the process of forgiveness a little easier.

5. Acknowledge Your Role

It's important to recognize that in any relationship, both parties play a role. Reflect on what part you might have played in the events that led to the divorce. This doesn't mean blaming yourself but rather understanding that we are all participants in our lives, not mere victims. By acknowledging your role, you take responsibility for your actions and begin seeing the situation more clearly.

6. Live in the Present

The past is behind you, and it no longer exists except in your memory. Constantly reliving past hurts keeps you trapped in a cycle of pain. Instead, bring your focus back to the present moment. What can you do today to bring joy and peace into your life? Focus on the here and now, and gradually, the past will lose its hold on you.

7. Invite Peace into Your Life

As you let go of the past, consciously invite peace into your life. Take deep breaths and imagine releasing the pain with each exhale. With each inhale, imagine breathing in peace, calm, and positivity. Let this practice become a part of your daily routine, gradually shifting your focus from the past to a more peaceful present.

Helping Children Understand and Accept Divorce

Divorce is a difficult experience not only for the couple involved but also for the children who are caught in the middle. The dissolution of a marriage can be confusing, frightening, and unsettling for a child, regardless of their age. It's important to help children understand the concept of divorce and guide them in accepting their new realities, ensuring that they feel supported and loved throughout the process.

Communicating the Reality of Divorce

The first step in helping children understand divorce is open and honest communication. Children need to know what is happening, why it's happening, and what it means for their lives. This conversation should be age-appropriate, clear, and delivered with empathy. It's important to reassure them that the divorce is not their fault, as children often internalize blame for the separation of their parents. Use simple language and be ready to answer their questions as truthfully as possible without overwhelming them with unnecessary details. The goal is to provide them with a basic understanding of what divorce is and why it's occurring while emphasizing that both parents still love them and will continue to be there for them.

Supporting Children in Accepting Their New Reality

Once children understand what divorce is, the next challenge is helping them accept the changes that come with it. Divorce often brings about significant shifts in a child's life—new living arrangements, changes in routines, and sometimes even new schools or neighborhoods. These changes can be overwhelming and difficult to process.

Parents can support their children by maintaining as much stability as possible. Consistent routines, regular communication, and the presence of familiar comforts can help ease the transition. It's also important to create a safe space for children to express their feelings, whether it's sadness, anger, or confusion. Encourage them to talk about what they're going through and validate their emotions.

Fostering Resilience and Adaptability

Divorce can be a challenging experience, but it also presents an opportunity to teach children about resilience and adaptability. Help them understand that while some things in their life may change, they have the strength and support to traverse these changes successfully. Encourage them to see the positive aspects of their new situation, whether it's having more quality time with each parent individually or the opportunity to develop new routines and traditions.

Additionally, be mindful of your own behavior and attitudes during this time. Children are perceptive, and they will take cues from how you handle the divorce. Demonstrating resilience, maintaining a positive outlook, and managing your emotions in a healthy way can provide a powerful example for your children.

Creating a Collaborative Parenting Environment

Co-parenting plays a crucial role in helping children accept the new reality of their parents' divorce. Even though the marriage has ended, the parenting relationship continues, and it's essential to work together to provide a stable, supportive environment for your children. Consistent rules, shared responsibilities, and a united approach to parenting can help children feel secure despite the changes around them.

Avoiding conflict in front of your children is also key. Witnessing parental conflict can exacerbate the emotional stress they are already experiencing. Strive to keep interactions with your co-parent respectful and focused on the well-being of your children.

Encouraging a Positive Outlook on the Future

Finally, help your children look forward to the future. Encourage them to see that while life may be different now, it can still be filled with love, happiness, and new experiences. Remind them that they have two parents who care deeply for them and that they will continue to be supported every step of the way.

In helping children understand and accept divorce, the focus should always be on love, communication, and stability. By providing these, you can help them navigate the complexities of divorce with resilience and grace, setting the foundation for a healthy adjustment to their new reality.

Healing from Trauma: A Personal Journey

Healing from trauma is not a linear path but one shaped by moments of vulnerability, resilience, and growth. As I made my way forward, therapy became a sanctuary where I confronted and released painful memories. It was there that I began to untangle the knots of my past and embrace the possibility of healing. Meditation and mindfulness practices helped me find peace within, grounding me in the present moment and helping me navigate the emotional storms that inevitably arose. The support of my family, friends, and mentors was invaluable. They offered constant encouragement and guidance, especially in times when I felt uncertain or overwhelmed. Their presence reminded me that I was not alone in my struggles, and their love helped me stay grounded as I worked through the healing process.

This journey was transformative; I no longer viewed myself as defined by my trauma but as someone who had grown through it. I came to understand that the experiences I had lived through, while painful, had contributed to shaping the person I had become. They made me stronger and more resilient, and ultimately, they inspired me to give back. I established counseling centers dedicated to helping others on their own journeys of healing, offering the same support and guidance that I had received.

Today, I stand as both a survivor and an advocate, using my experiences to show others that healing is possible, even after profound loss. Life, despite deep pain, can still be rich, fulfilling, and meaningful. I've learned that while our pasts shape us, they do not have to define us. We possess the power to rise above, grow, and create a life filled with hope, love, and purpose. Healing from the wounds of divorce is not about erasing scars but learning to live with them, transforming them into sources of strength. Forgiveness became my greatest act of self-love, allowing me to reclaim the parts of myself that pain had once taken. I stand not as a victim of my past but as a testament to the resilience that comes from surviving it.

As we conclude this journey together, I hope you have found strength and insight in these pages. Healing is not a destination but a journey, one that requires patience, self-compassion, and courage. For me, the journey has been transformative, not just in overcoming the wounds of my past but in finding my purpose through them. Today, I stand as someone who has turned pain into a mission: to help others discover their own strength and path to healing.

To anyone reading this: know that healing is possible. You are not defined by your past but by how you choose to move forward. Embrace the power within you to let go, to forgive, and to create a future filled with hope, love, and purpose. This is not just my story; it's evidence of the resilience that exists in all of us.

Thank you for allowing me to share my story with you. May your own journey be one of peace, strength, and hope.

www.ingramcontent.com/pod-product-compliance
Lightning Source LLC
Chambersburg PA
CBHW051726270125
20903CB00050B/899